Identifying and Su
the Dyslexic

Written by Carol Mellers
Illustrated by Lou Moore

Revised Edition

Part One: Identifying the Dyslexic Child

1. Dyslexia—a medical definition
2. What to look for
3. Diffficulties in language related skills

Dyslexia—A medical definition

Two types of dyslexia have been identified:

- ❏ **acquired**, i.e. as a result of brain injury due to accident, stroke, senility, Alzheimer's disease etc.
- ❏ **developmental**, i.e. where the child is born with dyslexia.

Possible causes of dyslexia:

- ❏ a different organisation of the brain, which does not lead to the efficient development of language processing and literacy skills. However, the effect is not all negative as there may be success in other areas e.g. technical skills, design, practical subjects, building etc.
- ❏ a different composition of the language components of the brain
- ❏ less efficient communication across the brain

Understanding the brain in relation to dyslexia:

- the **left hemisphere** of the brain is the logical side, primarily dealing with processing speech and language

- the **right hemisphere** is the visual, practical, intuitive side, with a smaller, less effective 'language' area

- communication between these two hemispheres is by means of nerve fibres

In dyslexics **it is thought** that there are varying abnormalities in this system, for example:

- the 'language areas' may be more evenly split between the left and right hemispheres as opposed to the normal brain where the language area is larger in the left hemisphere

- much of the language processing may be done in the less efficient right hemisphere

- the nerve fibres may be less efficient communicators

There are **two distinct groups of dyslexics** although all dyslexics are individuals with their own pattern of difficulties:

- **the left hemisphere type**, who make better use of the left side of the brain but who are not functioning totally efficiently. These are generally good at talking with reasonably well-developed language. They have less problems with reading but they often have poor motor control/co-ordination etc. They are often 'clumsy' and disorganised.

- **the right hemisphere type**, who can perform visual and spatial tasks well (jigsaws, design, lego, models, construction etc.) but who are often poor communicators with many language processing problems.

Facts and Figures

- 1 in 10 people are affected with dyslexia
- 70% of dyslexics are male
- 80% of dyslexics have a history of family problems

4

What to Look For

This section looks at early identification and the recognition of difficulties not immediately related to reading and writing.

The problems related to dyslexia often become apparent when the child starts to fail to acquire literacy skills at school, and falls behind the peer group. However, the condition manifests itself in many other ways, which if spotted earlier, can prevent failure.

It is very important to be aware that each child has his/her own pattern of strengths and weaknesses.

Early Identification

It is important to have as much background information as possible, concerning:

- ❏ birth
- ❏ early acquisition of speech
- ❏ development of physical skills, such as crawling, walking, feeding
- ❏ hearing

- ❏ general health
- ❏ development of a 'preferred' hand
- ❏ anxiety or frustration

Problems or delay in any of these areas may result in later difficulties with the acquisition of literacy skills at school.

Recognising Difficulties

Memory

Working or short-term memory is a particular difficulty for dyslexics. It affects individuals to different degrees, but can give rise to many of the other problems experienced, and referred to throughout this section.

The pupil with dyslexia may forget:
- ❏ equipment
- ❏ instructions
- ❏ notes home
- ❏ names
- ❏ information
- ❏ homework

S/He may also have difficulty putting to good use, and manipulating, information already stored in long term memory.

Poor retention of information may lead to lack of concentration, restlessness and disruptive behaviour.

Difficulty sequencing:

It is common for dyslexics to have problems with putting things in their correct order like:

- ❏ days of the week
- ❏ seasons
- ❏ months of the year
- ❏ numbers
- ❏ letters
- ❏ events
- ❏ stories

Directional confusion:

Dyslexics often find it difficult to get their directions right, such as:

- ❏ up/down
- ❏ under/over
- ❏ left/right
- ❏ in front/behind etc.

Such confusions may lead to children experiencing difficulties finding their way around a building, a room, a book, a piece of paper e.g. 'Where do I start?'

Time

Time is a difficult concept for most young children. Learning to tell the time is a complex skill, acquired at different stages for individuals. However, the dyslexic child finds it more difficult, and has particular difficulty understanding the overall concept of time.

This can be recognised by the confusion s/he experiences in:

- ❏ remembering what day to bring particular equipment
- ❏ knowing what event follows another e.g. assembly follows registration
- ❏ understanding terms such as 'yesterday' and 'tomorrow'
- ❏ appreciating time spans e.g. last week, next weekend
- ❏ knowing what time of the day it is e.g. 'Is it play time or home time?'

Mixed dominance

This is the lack of a distinct preference to use one hand for all activities giving an appearance of ambidexterity. Further investigations can be undertaken. Check for the preferred ear (e.g. for the telephone) and eye (telescope). A confusion of right and left preferences may be related to difficulty in the efficient processing of language.

Poor concentration

Dyslexics often find it difficult to concentrate for any length of time due to:

- ❒ short attention span and short memory span
- ❒ tiredness/restlessness
- ❒ poor auditory discrimination

Co-ordination

Some dyslexics have difficulty with basic co-ordination leading to problems with:

- ❒ dressing and coping with buttons and laces
- ❒ throwing, catching, kicking
- ❒ hopping, skipping, running, jumping
- ❒ colouring, tracing, drawing, writing

This is least likely to apply to all dyslexics as many are skilled in physical activities such as P.E. and Technology. On the whole, however, they favour individual sports, such as athletics lacking the organisational skills to work as a part of a team.

Stress

Dyslexic children are quite often concious of their difficulties. They see their friends succeeding in activities where they are failing but they do not understand the reason for their failure. Consequently they often feel sure that they should achieve the same success as others. As a result they become confused and frustrated. The child may respond to this situation in a number of different ways for example:

- ❒ showing a determination to battle against all odds
- ❒ becoming physically exhausted
- ❒ becoming emotionally exhausted
- ❒ showing nervous anxiety, leading to possible 'school phobia' and other signs of stress e.g. bed wetting
- ❒ becoming shy and introverted
- ❒ becoming aggressive

Unfortunately the parents of a dyslexic child become equally worried about their child's failure, and may quite unintentionally pass on their own anxieties to the child. Therefore a good relationship between home and school is essential at such times.

Teachers need to be aware of the stress factors at home and the behaviour patterns which may only be apparent out of school. Parents need to be aware of the problems at school and of how everyone can work together to make the learning experience more accessible and pleasurable.

Difficulties in Language Related Skills

This section looks at the sort of difficulties experienced by dyslexic children in school, especially in relation to National Curriculum English, Key Stages 1 and 2.

☐   Speaking

☐   Reading

☐   Writing

It should be noted that many pupils will still be experiencing these difficulties at secondary school (Key Stage 3), where it will be particularly important that written material is suitably differentiated, and suitable teaching styles employed to meet their needs.

Speaking (Attainment Target 1)

It is generally accepted that most dyslexic pupils express themselves well orally. It is often this skill which helps the teacher to recognise the potential of the pupil when it is less apparent in written work.

Closer analysis of a dyslexic's oral contribution may reveal sound knowledge of the subject, a lively imagination or ingenious originality, but there may be the following weaknesses:

- inefficient sentence construction
- inappropriate vocabulary (including malapropisms, and spoonerisms)
- poor sequencing skills
- lack of coherence
- inclusion of much irrelevant information
- lack of precision

These characteristics of the dyslexic's speech raise difficulties for the programmes of study for Attainment Target 1 (Speaking and Listening) which require that pupils make "themselves clear through organising what they say and choosing words with precision..."

Reading (Attainment Target 2)

Difficulties may arise early on with:

- acquiring a sight vocabulary
- learning phonics
- blending letter sounds
- distinguishing between similar looking letters or words
- distinguishing between similar sounding letters or words
- identifying a word in a line, or on a page, of print
- recognising the same word again on the same page
- following lines of print without losing place

- making connections between similar letter patterns
- applying acquired knowledge to a 'new' word
- reading aloud
- abstracting meaning from texts
- using texts to reach conclusions, predict outcomes etc.

It is soon apparent how this may affect coping with some of the programmes of study:

Levels 1 to 3 (Key Stage 1/2)

- recognition of familiar words in simple texts
- use of knowledge of letters and sound-symbol relationships in order to read words and establish meaning when reading aloud
- use of more than one strategy, such as phonic, graphic, syntactic and contextual, in reading unfamiliar words
- reading of a range of texts fluently and accurately
- use of knowledge of alphabet to locate books and find information

Level 4 (Key Stages 2–4)

- beginning to use inference and deduction
- referring to the text when explaining views
- **locates** and uses ideas and information

Writing (Attainment Target 3)

The majority of dyslexic pupils experience difficulty committing information and ideas to paper. Programmes of Study for Attainment Target 3 at Key Stages 1 & 2 (levels 1 to 4) make reference to:

- conventional letter formation
- legible handwriting styles
- common spelling patterns
- remembering correct spellings
- alphabetical order
- chronological writing
- punctuation
- planning an ordered framework
- choice of vocabulary

If we look at the typical features of a piece of work of a child with dyslexia, we can see immediately how the pupil may be failing in these areas at an early age:

- poor letter formation
- illegible handwriting
- many crossings out
- inconsistent or bizarre spelling
- poor sequencing of events
- lack or inappropriate use of punctuation
- inconsistent use of capital letters
- lack of organisation of ideas/thoughts
- lack of structure/planning
- omission of words
- poor sentence construction
- inappropriate choice of vocabulary
- inaccurate copying
- inability to identify their own mistakes

These traits may still be apparent at Key Stages 3 and 4, when pupils are expected to communicate independently, and at length, in the written form, for a wide range of purposes.

By this time pupils may be well aware of their short-comings and experiencing a sense of failure and frustration, often exacerbated by the fact that they are judged on their written performance, often finding themselves in lower sets or streams than their intellectual potential merits.

Part Two: Supporting the Dyslexic Child

Some useful strategies

Some Useful Strategies

In General

Be positive:

- offer praise and encouragement for success and effort
- recognise and reward practical achievement
- listen to and accept, with equal merit, verbal explanations

Be sympathetic and understanding:

- be aware of the problems leading to the forgotten homework, the lost letter, the missed information about a sports fixture
- recognise the confusion and frustration of the pupil and avoid situations which increase pressure
- do not correlate variability of performance with lack of effort
- recognise the amount of effort required for a dyslexic pupil to achieve a small quantity of good work
- recognise the restlessness and lack of concentration resulting from this effort and realise that this is not laziness

Instructions (verbal and written):

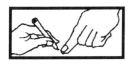

- check they are understood
- give one at a time
- present instructions in a clear manageable form
- check homework instructions are written clearly and legibly
- be prepared to write down legibly such instructions for the pupil

Length of tasks:

- match these to the pupil's concentration span, extending them gradually
- give short tasks with a definite and achievable end in sight
- allow 'breaks' or 'time out', e.g. allow pupils to clean the board or do an errand as some sort of movement can be a great help

Practical Help
Copying

This is often an area of weakness; a child appears to be careless, but is often experiencing short term memory or spatial difficulties e.g. loss of place, jumping a line. When this happens:

- do not criticise mistakes
- sit the pupil near the board
- if possible allow him or her to copy from a card/sheet next to him
- be patient with slow speed
- do not penalise unfinished work
- do not rely on important notes/instructions being copied accurately
- allow clearly presented typed photocopies to be provided . While others are copying, time can be spent reading through, highlighting important points, discussing difficulties with the teacher etc.

Notetaking

- allow typed notes
- give a taped version; some pupils will be able to take notes from this, with less pressure—but allow time or allow pupil to take a copy of the tape. A typed **and**

a taped version is the best aid to revision for many pupils.

- a lap top computer may help some pupils

Written work

Allow alternative means of recording information:

- oral
- taped
- typed/word processed
- video recorded
- illustrated etc.

Reading

Reading may be a problem area for pupils but this is not always necessarily so.

The good 'mechanical' reading skill of some dyselxics can, however, be misleading. They may have difficulty with the meaning of texts and with advanced comprehension skills, such as deduction, inference, prediction.

Reading aloud is almost always a difficulty, and consequently a cause of embarrassment and anxiety.

It is important to:

- check the suitability of written texts
- read to the pupil where practical e.g. maths problems and instructions
- allow taped material to be used
- do not ask the pupil to read aloud in front of others unless s/he wants to

N.B. Failure to read the instructions or understand the question can be the cause of failure in areas of the curriculum where a pupil might otherwise achieve great success e.g. practical subjects, science, maths.

Learning to Read (Primary School)

Praise and encouragement are very necessary.

It is important that the child's interest in books is nurtured and maintained. This can be best achieved through paired or shared reading, so that the material can be at an appropriate interest level.

Learning to read is, for these children, a separate activity from reading for pleasure. 'The more they read, the more they improve' is less appropriate than 'the more they read, the more they fail'.

Reading will need to be taught by means of a highly structured, systematic and multisensory programme, ideally by trained Learning Support Teachers.

A 'reading' book is not an essential part of such a course, but if one is to be used in order for the pupil to feel the same as his peers, then it must be at such a level that s/he succeeds. 'Sounding out' should be avoided with unfamiliar or forgotten words being provided. A particular word may be chosen afterwards to learn, or to relate back to a teaching point, or for its common letter pattern.

Cross Curricula Implications (Secondary School)

Many text books and worksheets are inaccessible to these pupils, not only due to readability, but also presentation.

Pupils can lose their place, or suffer from the blurring of print which is either too small or too closely spaced.

Too much information on one page can often be daunting. Where there are charts, diagrams, graphs and illustrations, pupils often have difficulty finding their way round the page, and relating the appropriate piece of written information to the illustration.

They can also have difficulty reading handwritten text.

Worksheets will need to be:

- clearly printed
- well spaced
- with clearly labelled diagrams/illustrations
- at an appropriate reading level
- taped

Spelling

Do:

- give lists of useful words, e.g. for a topic, or subject, **typed** for sticking in appropriate exercise book
- provide the pupil with a 'dictionary' divided into topic areas
- encourage use of 'spelling dictionaries' such as 'ACE Spelling Dictionary' 'The Pergammon Dictionary of Perfect Spelling' and spellcheckers, such as the 'Franklin'

Do not:

- ask the pupil to look up a spelling in an ordinary dictionary. How do you find it if you cannot spell it?
- do not comment on or correct misspellings, except those which have been taught or provided

The teaching of spelling, like reading, needs to be structured and multi-sensory, and preferably taught by a specially trained teacher.

Some useful tips:

- group words together which are regular, both phonically and visually and can be presented in a multi-sensory way.
- give irregular words individually, to be learnt as a whole word
- teach spelling rules e.g. for adding suffixes
- employ mnemonics or other memory strategies e.g. **B**irds **E**at **C**aterpillars **A**nd **U**pset **S**tupid **E**arwigs
- encourage syllable division e.g. cir-cum-fer-ence

Marking:

- mark positively i.e. praise and reward that which is done well
- judge content separately from presentation
- incorrect spellings could be pointed out by **underlining in pencil**, allowing the pupil the opportunity to correct and rub out the pencil mark (see 'Spelling' section for which words to pinpoint)
- avoid the disfiguration of pupil's work by excess of red ink

If you have difficulty reading a pupil's work, either ask him to read it to you, or better still allow him to record or type it in the first place.

Word Processing

For those children who have experienced years of failure with written work, the keyboard is a welcome relief. In spite of slow typing speed dyslexic pupils are likely to complete an assignment in less time, taking into consideration the fact that they will not need to rewrite the whole thing several times.

Proof reading one's own handwriting, only to turn it into an even more unpresentable scrawl is not a satisfying task. However, to be able to correct it on a word processor, with the aid of a spellchecker, the capability of manoeuvring sentences, adding, and deleting (without trace, smudge/or red pen) at the touch of a button, and finishing with a highly presentable piece of work, is both rewarding and motivating.

Where the physical act of handwriting is the problem area the keyboard is an ideal alternative. Some pupils experience an alleviation of anxiety when the keyboard is placed at their finger tips rather than the pen and paper. Some pupils' spelling noticeably improves (without the spellchecker!) when they can communicate via a word processor.

Given these facts, it is important, therefore, to use the word processor for:

- drafting
- planning
- redrafting

and **not** for slowly and painstakingly copying out already drafted, corrected, and rewritten work, which has often taken hours of anguish and hard work.

Remember—many dyslexics are inaccurate copiers. What could be worse than all the time spent copying out only to be told there are more mistakes on the typed copy than on the original.

If it is not feasible to let the child do the whole piece of work, from the start, on the word processor and he or she has produced a good but unattractive hand written piece of work, perhaps a volunteer typist could copy it up to show that it is valued.

A note of caution.

A word processor is not the solution to everyone's problems, and there are those who do not find it useful. It is helpful to provide keyboard and word processing training.